Instant Money Spells

Money Magick that works! Easy spells for beginners learning money magick

by

Gabriel Archer

Copyright © 2014 Gabriel Archer

All rights reserved.

ISBN-13: 978-1500115289
ISBN-10: 1500115282

PREFACE

Do you want more money? Are you looking for easy spells for beginners?

Instant Money Spells is written by a professional occultist of over 20 years experience so it's full of spells that work!

The easy money spells and potions in Instant Money Spells takes the most powerful occult systems and streamlines them into an effortless, effective method for attracting an abundance of money.

The money magick spells for beginners are real spells that work and cover how to cast spells, the items you need and more importantly how to get solid results - FAST!

Whether you want emergency money or a strong financial future, spells for money, in particular spells for beginners are what you are looking for. The easy money spells and potions in Instant Money Spells this mix of ancient talismans and modern secrets which get wealth flowing into your life - TODAY!

Table of Contents

The Endless Possibilities of Magick	4
Reasons for Using Money Magick	8
Further Information on Money Spells	13
Why Magick Can Increase Your Overall Wealth	16
What's Your Part in Making Magick Work?	19
Why Magick is Nothing to Fear	21
What Sort of Person Finds Success through Magick?	27
Quit Blocking Your Own Attractive Energies	30
Can Visualization Really Work?	33
How Visualization Can Enhance Your Magick	37
Performing Your Rituals Regularly	41
Customizing Your Money Magick	43
Crafting the Best Spells You Can	47
Some Cautions Regarding Money Magick	55
Money Talismans	57
The Money Jar	59
High John's Bag of Luck	62
Easy Tonka Bean Talisman	64

Money Magnet	66
Magick by Moonlight	68
When One Door Closes…	70
Finance by Five	72
Welcoming New Wealth	74
Candle Magick	76
Pay Your Bills	78
Elemental Earnings	82
Wax-Covered Token of Wealth	85
Ringing in New Tidings	87
Sweet Dreams of Success	89
Money from the Darkness	92
Simple Money Magick	95
Visualization Bath	97
Harvest Husk Wealth Spell	99
Powerfully Potent Potpourri	101
Planting the Seeds of Success	104
The Five-Knotted Banknote	107
No-Fail Money Spells	109

Apple and Athame	111
Attraction Energy Tea	114
The Jar of Hope	116
Conclusion	119

The Endless Possibilities of Magick

Magick is a word at which some of us have balked in the past. This is when we were still naïve as to its meaning.

When someone speaks to you of "witches" casting mystical spells, it is easy to think they've gotten off on the wrong stop halfway between Hogwarts and the loony bin.

Others of us may think them simply foolish, while yet others think magick to be the practice of fakery and parlor tricks.

The misunderstanding arises from the fact that the word itself is used in two different ways, which some people differentiate by their spelling.

This means that the traditional spelling of "magic" is used primarily for illusionists such as Harry Houdini or David Blaine.

When the spelling "magick" is used, it references something entirely different.

Magick creates a universal connection between people and the energies surrounding them to help them accomplish greater things than unfocused willpower can achieve. It can harness one's hopes and dreams into the power to make them a reality.

To some, it is an active manifestation of prayer. By connecting our energy to that of the earth, we strengthen our ambitions and attract what we need to enhance our way of life.

Some may think of this as increasing our luck, but this is not quite accurate. When viewing things spiritually, you will find it hard to see anything as simple fortune.

Everything has its purpose, and magick can help you discover yours.

We are essentially walking containment units for magickal energy. Those who believe in specters believe that they are the manifestation of this energy after leaving its vessel. It is the focus on this power within ourselves, and the belief that all beings (and even objects) possess this power, that makes magick possible.

As previously stated, magick is essentially the connection between ourselves and that which surrounds us.

The word "witch," despite its negative connotations, is simply a descriptive term for those who have learned to harness these connections over time and practice.

Note that the belief aspect of magick, the notion that we are not the only ones in possession of internal strength, is a significant part of how it works.

Through belief, even those who do not practice the craft itself may benefit from its teachings. This is because personal items can be charged by others.

So long as one believes in the power of the charmed item in their possession, it will work for them even if they had no part in the ritual of enchantment.

Those who do not believe that they will receive the good fortune promised to them will likely yield no results, or even possibly negative ones.

In short, magick is not for the cynic; however, those who believe will find in it a haven for all of their worldly desires.

The dividends promised by firm belief in the reality of magick and all it can deliver will prove time and time again that our lives can carry more purpose than we ever dreamed.

We simply need to give things a little push in the right direction.

Reasons for Using Money Magick

Many shrug off the belief that money can't buy happiness.

To some, it is not about physically possessing money but about the possibilities offered by a better job and financial security.

If you're seeking more than a few extra bills, money magick may be right up your alley.

Money magick is nothing new. Wherever there have been people, there has always been someone in want of more than they have.

There are several negative beliefs surrounding magick, not to mention magick used to increase personal gains, but that does not mean the practice is inherently bad. There is nothing wrong or evil about wanting more, so long as your intentions are pure.

Not everyone has pure intentions, but if this concerns you than your ethics are most likely on the right side of things.

Unfortunately, there are those who are less than wholesome in their monetary ambitions, so always be careful about with whom you share your knowledge in this field.

Always ask yourself why you (or they) are seeking more money in the first place. This will provide some insight as to the morals behind the decision to invoke magick in financial endeavors.

Once you have decided that your intentions are pure, it is time to decide whether you will be performing these money rituals yourself or consulting someone more experienced in the art of casting.

When performing magick, you are not tearing open the skies to change the world as it is, but rather influencing the future in a way that suits your needs. The "witch" that you might seek to help you is not some frightening figure from Oz.

They are simply a person who believes in healing and helping others to fulfill their dreams and foretell their fate.

Magick can be an everyday practice, not just a tool which is used when a need or want is at its peak.

Magick can improve the happiness and wellbeing of a person who is dissatisfied with their current position and disenchanted with life in general.

Someone who practices magick on a daily basis may find themselves more attuned to nature and the people around them, more secure about their physical and mental health, more aware of what their future holds and much more generally happy about where they are in life.

These are only a few of the vital life changes made possible by daily magick use.

Along with love spells (which have their own set of ethics to uphold), money spells are in high demand.

This has always been so, but the current economic climate has had an immeasurable impact on the frequency with which money spells are used. This means that the demand does not stem from basic avarice but from an actual need to increase one's funds.

If you are one of those who is in actual need of money magick to subsist, then paying someone to do the ritual for you may seem a bit counterintuitive.

Luckily, you can cast any number of spells on your own, so long as you maintain faith in yourself and in the rites you are performing.

Now that you know you are safe from wrongdoing and that magick can improve your life if you will let it, you are nearly ready to begin your journey into the spiritual realm to seek wealth and good fortune in all facets of life.

But don't set up for your ritual just yet! Your journey begins with some further education.

Further Information on Money Spells

As you've already been made aware, there is no inherent harm or danger presented by the use of magick for financial gain. After all, who knows? You may end up with more than you intended and find a way to help more than just yourself.

This is one way in which money spells can breed more than just financial wealth. Increasing your karmic wellbeing may even strengthen your connection to the energies around you, making future magickal endeavors even more fruitful.

Magick is a long-standing tradition which has been present since the ancient days of Greece, Egypt, and even Mesopotamia.

While many new age practices tend to be more Germanic in their origins, the point is that magickal activities and the morals regarding them have been around for much longer than you can imagine. Similar beliefs have transcended cultural boundaries in terms of race, nationality, and even religion.

While religion may seem to be the most notable boundary transcended, social class is more germane to the discussion of money spells.

Some people picture those who use the craft for financial gains as being of a lesser economic class and likely in need of a job, but the truth is that even highly successful individuals utilize money magick to ensure the continuation of their success. Even those who use alternative means to gain their wealth may use such methods of increasing their fortune.

For instance, professional gamblers may use numbers and probabilities to process information when making a bet, but many of them are still among the most superstitious people you will ever meet. This is to their benefit, as they are already inclined to believe in the magick they employ through mantras and "lucky" (read as "charmed") objects.

Ask any one of these people, and they will assure you that the magick they have employed to build and maintain their financial security was vital to the success of their monetary pursuits.

Money spells have helped debtors, job-seekers, lottery players and the upwardly mobile. Some have made a great deal of money all at once, while others have achieved all-around success in their careers. The best part of money magick is that not only is it effective, but it is often a very simple engagement.

Usually those who cast spells for money are in something of a rush to see the fruits of their efforts, so it comes as no surprise that most spells are tailored to this desire.

Thanks to the work of early civilizations over thousands of years, you can perform your spell with just a little bit of prep work and maybe a basic incantation.

Why Magick Can Increase Your Overall Wealth

We've discussed people maintaining their wealth and earning new careers. But is it possible to actually become rich as the result of using magick rituals and spell casting?

You'll be pleasantly surprised to learn that this is indeed the case. While the concentration put into money spells can create and strengthen ambition, this is not all that magick has to offer.

Magickal energies are also good for attraction. This means that, in addition to turning you into the type of person who merits success, magick can also actively bring good things your way.

Now, you're probably thinking that you've heard this promise before. You've probably seen it in your spam folder more than anywhere else.

Anonymous strangers are constantly telling you:

GET RICH QUICK!

EARN $$$ FROM YOUR VERY OWN HOME!

MAKE BANK IN MINUTES (AND INCREASE YOUR SEX DRIVE)!

WE'LL PAY YOU THOUSANDS JUST TO BROWSE THE WEB!

Even those skeptical of magick must admit that these promises sound ten times as ridiculous as the notion that harnessing your internal energy can mean good things for you.

You've probably met a successful person who used magick and regarded them as simply superstitious. But have you ever met someone who got rich by clicking links on their web browser?

Some of the wealthier people you know probably have a certain quality about them that you can't quite put your finger on yet seems to factor into their success. This quality is essentially what you stand to gain from the attraction energies provided by money spells.

And there is the primary purpose of the basic money spell. Not simply to increase your drive, but to enhance your energies of attraction.

If you are open to these energies, they may bring success to more areas of your life than just your pocketbook.

What's Your Part in Making Magick Work?

You have probably gathered by now that your own personal beliefs are key to making magickal energies work.

As with any type of ritual, you must cultivate the proper thoughts and beliefs to fit your specific purpose. While the spells may be written for you, only you can put the necessary energy and concentration into them that makes them work.

The people mentioned in the last chapter who seem to naturally find success at every turn are actually gifted with the inclination to let success find them.

This is the sort of mind-set and control of power that you will gain through using money spells, but you must also have a fair amount of it going in.

In other words, you are basically investing your energies and reaping greater dividends over time.

No one else can do this for you. You have nothing to lose by putting your energies into magick that will better you and your life circumstances with no risk of harm to yourself or others.

When all it takes is a proper belief system, there is no doubt that YOU HAVE WHAT IT TAKES to achieve success and fortune. With some practice, you may eventually even learn to write your own spells so that you can always gain precisely what you want.

There is nothing worldly you can't achieve with this type of magick. Think of these spells as "belief incantations," wherein the primary tool is simply faith that you can have what you most desire.

Why Magick is Nothing to Fear

Many people are afraid of magick. While this is in no small part due to a fear of the unexplained, part of the blame also goes to those who practice magick themselves.

Those new to the path are warned against treacherous missteps that may shake the foundation of everything they aim to work toward.

Rubbish! In some instances, maybe these warnings are fair. But in this case, you should not equate trying to make a little extra cash with reciting the Necronomicon.

Rituals geared toward money-making are not inherently good or evil. If your intentions are ill, that may be one thing, but the sheer act of accumulating wealth has no bearing on your ethical standing whatsoever.

The only way you stand to suffer harm is if you build up karmic negativity or simply don't know what you are doing. Since you're currently educating yourself on proper magick use, and are presumably aiming to keep your morals in check, you should not let this worry you.

Magick is a driving force, so think of it in these terms like an automobile. Those who commit acts of reckless driving or vehicular homicide are prone to suffer consequences.

Those who practice defensive driving and use their car as a simple means of transportation are not. And at heart, isn't that all you're doing?

Aren't you merely using money spells as a method of transporting yourself on the road to a better life? Why should this be something to fear?

The major difference between money magick and the automobile is that the automobile functions on its own.

You simply switch the ignition and the engine does the rest of the work. Magick is more like the car Fred Flintstone uses; magick requires you to work.

It makes sense if you think about it for all of two seconds. You don't perform a spell with the goal of getting a promotion and then spend your days dragging your feet. This is where harm might actually be done.

Picture it this way.

Imagine you cast a spell for a better job, and the attraction energies you put out into the ether open up your employer's eyes to the rigor you've been putting into your work thus far.

Now you, complacent in your belief that a promotion will simply fall on your lap, start slacking off.

Not only will you not get that promotion, but you may lose any chance of advancement in the future (or worse, your current employment). Throwing errant magick around in this way is a bit like trying to drive your car by closing the garage door and then idling in the exhaust fumes.

In other words, you need to look at how things got to the point that you had to rely on magick in the first place.

If you're having trouble paying the bills then a money spell might help you for now, but you might need to seek a long-term solution by changing homes or jobs.

Maybe your boss will never respect you enough to promote you, but you might be able to find employment in an atmosphere you find more enjoyable and where you are also more respected.

The spells you cast will help to open these windows of opportunities, but only you can open your own mind enough to see them when they are presented.

Always seek something better, and seek it actively. Magick can help you achieve anything, but only with your cooperation.

One key word of caution is to follow the advice you've been learning from folklore since you were a toddler: "Be careful what you wish for."

Simply put, don't ask for too much or too little. If you only work on making enough to subsist, then you will remain in a similar cycle to that which you have already experienced, with the added cost of ritual supplies.

If you ask for too much, you may get nothing. Worse yet, you may find yourself with too many responsibilities to manage and spread yourself thin to the point that your increased wealth is more of a burden than a blessing.

For the time being, focus on stability.

Once you've achieved this stability, you can focus on further increasing your earnings. It never hurts to have goals for something better. You may have seen self-help articles on finance and success reference a "dream board." Maybe it was called by a different name, but the basic premise is to have a corkboard adorned with representations of things you'd like to attain in the future.

Believe it or not, the maintenance of such a board is its own manifestation of attraction energy. But don't just dream it. Harness your energy and see it through to fruition.

Most importantly, enjoy yourself. Once you've reached a level of stability and you're simply trying to seek out a more enjoyable lifestyle, don't feel as if you've fallen pretty to some horrific brand of avarice.

Wanting more out of life doesn't mean you're Ebenezer Scrooge. It means you're human, and that's a wonderful thing to be.

What Sort of Person Finds Success through Magick?

It's already been mentioned multiple times that the strength of your beliefs will have a large effect on whether or not money spells will work for you, as well as affecting the speed at which they work.

The issue of concentration, however, warrants further discussion.

The more you question the ability of magick to deliver what you want, the more difficult it will be to lend your full concentration to the spell you're working.

This means that, albeit subconsciously, you are emitting negative energies that will resist the very things you aim to attract. When you think about it, magick is basically one big self-fulfilling prophecy.

Remember earlier, when I said that those who regularly practice magick are more attuned with the universe? Well those who are out of tune are going to have a much harder time of getting what they want.

If you cast a spell while secretly expecting it to fail, then you can't be too surprised when you don't get what you want.

You're essentially spitting into the winds of fate and then complaining about the blowback.

The solution is to have confidence in the spell you are working, for there is no point in working a spell without faith.

This requires a somewhat meditative state when performing your money magick rituals. You have to be able to visualize what you want while keeping any and all negative thoughts completely out of the picture.

This is easier said than done, and will likely take some practice. If you've never experienced the type of stability you're hoping to gain, then it can be hard to imagine what it's like to live that sort of life; however, once you have this process of visualization nailed, you may find yourself surrounded by an aura of peace before the magick has even taken effect.

This is precisely what you are aiming for, as it means you have cultivated the right sort of belief system necessary to success.

One simple means of increasing your powers of concentration is to use a visual aid in your magickal process. For instance, candles are already a primary tool used in spell casting.

If you are able to visualize the life you want while focusing your eyes on the flame, without looking away in doubt, then you are ready to start experimenting with more advanced techniques.

Quit Blocking Your Own Attractive Energies

Many of the roadblocks touched upon to this point have revolved around doubt, lack of self-confidence, fear and lack of focus.

These things must be eliminated if you are to have any hope of achieving anything through magick.

Some people believe that fear is at the root of all negative actions and emotions. The question, then, is fear of what?

The answers are abundant, but they can be summed up in general by one simple word: failure.

To many, failure is the manifestation of losing control. Nearly all practitioners of magick are attempting to gain control over some aspect of their lives. The problem is that, as we have witnessed throughout history, obsession with control leads some people to a very dark place, and this is where your ambitions may become less than well-meaning.

This may be at the heart of the tendency which we have previously discussed of most magick instructors to cultivate fear in their students. They are instilled with worry that they may be judged for using magick, or for wanting more control over their lives in the first place.

They are experiencing guilt over their quest for power, possibly due to malicious intent on their part, and they are projecting that negativity onto you. DO. NOT. LET. THEM!

They may be doing this intentionally, and they may not, but that is beside the point. The point is that desires for money, love, and other forms of good fortune arise out of basic human instinct.

The quest for power over these things is not unnatural; in fact, these instinctual desires might be considered at least partially responsible for the continuation of the human race. It is only when the struggle for control becomes excessive that a person's morals begin to falter, and this is the sort of self-centered fear of which you must be mindful.

Do not let the faults of others sway you from pursuing your own spiritual growth. When you have achieved a true mystic oneness with your surroundings, you will be able to admit that you are deserving of the life to which you aspire.

You will know the difference between right and wrong, and trust that you are in the right.

This trust in yourself is vital, for without it you will never achieve true control over your life, and your attempts at harnessing the true promises of magick will be for naught.

Can Visualization Really Work?

Visualization is sometimes an understated practice, possibly due to the fact that it simply sounds too easy. It's hard to believe that simply imagining a desired circumstance can lend any power to its actualization. Yet people have used this seemingly simple tool to attain wealth, respect, and even improved health.

Why? How? Certainly, some sort of mischief is afoot.

Lucky for you, friend, this is not the case. Visualization really is a valuable tool, and the best part is that you've had it in your toolbox since you were a child.

The only drawback is that the disillusionment of adulthood tends to impact the imagination, so you will need to refocus your energies on rebuilding this power to its maximum effectiveness.

You've probably heard multiple times in your life that "seeing is believing." This is the ideal to which you must cling tightly if you are to achieve proper visualization.

In this case, the beliefs you want to maintain revolve around your personal aptitude in achieving your heart's desires. You have probably achieved this type of focus in the past, sometimes quite unknowingly.

Have you ever imagined striking up a conversation with an interesting person and immediately found yourself compelled to do so? Have you ever focused on the promise of better health to motivate yourself through a workout routine?

Visualization operates under a principle as basic as these examples, yet can be used to achieve much more.

The effectiveness of visualization lies in your ability to visualize your desired circumstance with absolute conviction. If you're seeking extra money for a vacation to Cabo San Lucas, for instance, try picturing every aspect of your intended destination.

If you can close your eyes and see the beach, smell the salt of the ocean, feel the sun on your back, hear the gulls above you, and taste the brine in the air, then you have experienced total meditative immersion and are much more likely to work toward your goal.

This is clearly much different than simply saying that you want something and hoping that it comes to you.

The key here to this sort of visualization is that you must place a limitless emphasis on sensory stimuli. If you can visualize your life with an open heart and open mind, then you can live that life in the same fashion.

There are a few ways to make this easier on yourself, which include:

- Calm your mind and relax your body before you begin.

- Utilize every sense you have in forming your meditative vision.

- Try to visualize your desires as thoroughly and realistically as possible.

- Filter out unwanted thoughts and images; this is YOUR vision.

- Go for the gold. The more bright, welcoming, and satisfying the images are, the more motivated you will be to turn them into reality.

- Don't be all business! This can be a fun exercise if you'll let it.

How Visualization Can Enhance Your Magick

"I visualize things in my mind before I have to do them. It's like having a mental workshop." - ***Jack Youngblood.***

"If you can dream it, you can do it." – ***Walt Disney***

There is NOTHING that you can't see with your mind's eye. Even some scientists are coming around to the idea that visualizing one's goals can show promising results for the wellbeing of body and mind.

While it may seem as if science has only recently begun to latch on, this does not mean the idea itself is new.

All walks of life from prominent business moguls to some of the bigger names in Hollywood have utilized these practices for many years.

Following the tips provided in the last chapter will increase the effectiveness of this great tool. Calmness and relaxation go a long way toward enhancing your efforts. In order to filter out unwanted stimuli, try to keep your eyes closed and your hearing concentrated on your own breaths or heartbeat.

As you feel your mind and body beginning to unify (the edges of your skin should become somewhat tingly, and you may find yourself feeling lighter), allow the image of your desires flow into your mind.

Wherever you want your mind's eye to take you, whatever you want to be doing there, try to make it as real as you can. Do not let it be just a faraway dream, but a sensation that changes your body as well as your mind.

If you are someplace sunny, you should actually feel as if your body is becoming warmer. Most likely, it will be.

This has a great effect not only on the way you see things, but the way they truly are. By creating the reality of your dreams within your own mind, you have discovered what it is like to live the life you've always wanted.

If it helps, think of this as a sort of role-play in which you are the main character and the goal is to explore your future. As you grow better at this practice, you may start to find yourself living out these "fantasies" in the physical realm.

The greater your goals, the more work it will take at perfecting this exercise to make them a reality. Never think that just because you've managed a single immersive meditation that you have completely set the wheels in motion.

You still need to be greasing those wheels in the real world, and this may take some time. Continue your visualizations often until they have come to pass.

Not only will repeated visualization increase the likelihood of getting what you want, but you will become better at it with practice. As such, you may find that it takes even less time to see your visions before your eyes instead of just within your mind.

Performing Your Rituals Regularly

We as humans have an unfortunate tendency to harbor numerous dreams and desires while also practicing an aversion to anything which is good for us.

We get just a little too tired to exercise, a little too stressed to meditate, and a little too pessimistic to pursue our goals actively.

If you find yourself in such a rut, you need to claw your way out immediately. You will often find that there is a deeper cause than any of which you are aware.

Maybe you are experiencing a bout of depression or anxiety that you just haven't fully recognized.

This can happen for any number of reasons. No matter what they may be, once you have become aware of them there is no excuse for not bettering the situation.

There are many solutions, but the continuation of anti-spiritual thinking is certainly not one of them.

Maybe you have heard the axiom "nothing changes if nothing changes." YOU are that change. You know that daily practice of ritual magick and visualization can help you, so follow the advice of one of the most spiritual men who ever lived and be the change you want to see.

Most importantly, never lose hope. The most positive changes you can see in your life will not happen overnight, but good things will come to you if you work toward them and are receptive to them.

Customizing Your Money Magick

Hopefully you have been paying attention and have come to full awareness that patience is one of the greatest virtues you will need to see your life improved by money magick, as is the desire to work for what you want.

You can combine these positive attributes by customizing your own spells. There is no "perfect" way to do this, but there is still some advice from which you can benefit.

Two credos have been repeated throughout these chapters which now bear strong reiteration. One is that your intentions are key to your success. The other is that you must check your negativity at the door and keep your morals in check at all times.

Do not attempt to over-complicate these rules. They must not be subverted in any way.

Decide when and where you will be performing your spell and make sure you have a focus for it. It always help to know as thoroughly as you can just what it is you are trying to achieve.

It doesn't matter when and where you choose to do it, so long as you feel at peace with this decision. Late at night, early in the morning, right around noon...whenever you best operate is the appropriate time.

You might want to do it somewhere by candlelight, or where you can see yourself in a mirror. It's entirely up to you.

I, for one, like to garden. So I tend to use either a fresh pot of seeds or a fully grown plant along with a token such as a money frog.

While some who use this method might like to work their magick with something fully grown to represent the growth they want, others (such as myself) might prefer something newly planted in fresh soil so that the plant's growth symbolizes the growth of finances we wish to achieve.

I use this growth as a source of meditative thought before, after, and often during my ritual. This ritual is not necessarily always the same, but consists of whatever I feel is important at the time to the cultivation of positive energy, such as candle magick, chanting/singing, and even dancing.

I say, "I will tend this plant as I tend my problem. As this plant grows, I will grow, and my problem will blossom into new life."

Notice that, in this simple promise, my problem is not some horrible evil to be vanished completely. It is a part of my personal development, my evolution.

Once this is done, I ponder on how I can further enhance the energies I have set in motion. Whether throwing myself into my current job or going on the hunt for a new one, I make sure that I am putting into action that toward which I have put my faith. I, like many others, also make some money from artwork and woodworking, so I may enhance my magick through these activities.

These activities increase both my monetary gain as well as my overall sense of calm. Anything that increases your belief that the magick will do its job is going to help enhance the power of the attraction energies you are creating.

Crafting the Best Spells You Can

So long as you put the proper energy and focus into it, crafting a good spell is not nearly as difficult as you might think.

This basic advice should help you out:

Intention
You cannot cast an effective spell without knowing what you hope to gain from it. Think hard on the manifestations you hope to achieve.

Be as specific as possible, so as to avoid disappointment. Ask for whatever you wish, so long as no harm is wished upon anyone.

If you cast your spell in the spirit of malice or even mischief, you will be subject to three-fold karmic law.

Correspondences

Every aspect of your spell corresponds to a greater power. The colors you use, the time at which the spell is performed, the specific items and ingredients you utilize, and even the emotion you put into the casting will all have great effect on the spell's power.

Choose these correspondences to best suit your needs. Also bear in mind the four essential elements: Earth, Air, Fire, Water. You may wish to choose one of these to be the main focus of your spell, and the above correspondences can all revolve around your chosen element.

Be vigilant when choosing herbs or candles to ensure that you are not putting the wrong energy concentration into your spell.

You will reap greater benefit if every item used in your magick is chosen to achieve the desired effect.

Since in this case you are focusing on money magick, you will most likely wish to use green-colored candles and stones or crystals.

One particularly effective quartz you might choose is aventurine. In terms of herb choices, you might consider using mint. It is also hard to go wrong with sage.

If you wish to consider timing and direction as well, perform your rites while facing north at the break of dawn.

Money Spells
Aside from sage and mint, you can also use honeysuckle and/or mugwort. Aside from simply using green candles and stones, you might consider using candles and tokens which have already been enchanted for your purpose.

There is no shortage of money candles available, and money frogs can be useful as well. As far as the elements are concerned, you will want to focus on Earth, which corresponds with the north.

Success Spells

There is a difference between money and success. While money corresponds with Earth, the color green, and the direction north, success corresponds with Fire, the color red, and the direction south.

The appropriate time is around noon, when the sun is highest in the sky. Appropriate ingredients include basil, bay laurel, nettle and rosemary.

The proper stones and crystals to use are those of a reddish hue, such as amber, carnelian, red jasper and tiger's eye.

Moon Phase

Aside from the time of day, you might also consider the time of month. More specifically, consider the phase that the moon is in.

This choice is somewhat intuitive. When you are trying to attract something such as money, success, love, or any other such abundance, you will want to cast your spell during a waxing moon (the movement from a New Moon to a Full Moon).

When you are attempting to banish something, such as negative energy or anything else that may inhibit your success, you will want to cast your spell during a waning moon (the movement from a Full Moon to a New Moon).

The Full Moon is the most powerful time for any spell, as the moon is at its peak energy. The second-best choice is during a New Moon. Both of these are effective, as they represent a transition period between lunar motions.

Wording
When many picture a proper incantation, they picture it in lyrical (usually rhyming) verse. This is not a necessity, but it does have its benefits.

The sheer act of writing a spell with such wording is a sign that great care and energy has been put into its making.

Such time and effort will almost always increase dividends in the long run, as there is a clear demonstration that you have spent your energy in considering the true purpose of your magick.

It also helps to put pen to paper so that the goal of the magick is "spelled" out clearly. You will then say the words aloud, preferably three times in succession, so that your words ring clearly and the universe will catch wind of them. This also helps to affirm your aims within your own mind.

If you are performing this rite for something that you actually need, consider putting a time frame in the wording.

Any detail you add to your spell will help to shield you from disappointing results. You do not want to perform magick for a promotion, only to receive a promotion which affects nothing but your title.

If you were casting a spell for something other than money or success, such as romance, you would not want to attract a creep. Always remember: Be careful what you wish for, because you just might get it!

Whether or not it is written down, end your casting with the phrase "So mote it be." This ancient phrase essentially means "So as I will it, so shall it be done."

In other words, it affirms the manifestation of your desires in the near future. In fact, "mote" is the past tense of "may," so in many ways this is like saying that good tidings are already on their way to you.

Spell Casting
No magick should ever be performed unless your heart is completely in it. If you do not care enough to give one second thought to the tools and ingredients you use, the words you speak, or the way in which the rite is performed, you cannot expect great promises from your spell. You must take this process seriously if you want serious results.

Bear in mind the fact that this magick will enhance your fortunes but will not manifest cash and material goods out of thin air. You must be willing to put in the same effort in the physical realm as you did in the spiritual.

Do not be one of countless people who complains of how futile it is to play the lottery when they have never purchased a ticket. After performing magick to achieve financial success, go out and do the work to ensure you see your desires fulfilled!

Some Cautions Regarding Money Magick

While money magick may lack the glamour and appeal associated with love magick, it is arguably much more useful. Everyone needs personal relationships, but nobody technically needs romance to survive in the same way they need financial stability.

Despite the fact that this form of magick may be more useful, do not expect that to mean that its effects will be immediate. Money doesn't grow on trees, nor does it fall from the sky, and no amount of magick will cause either of these things to happen.

Sometimes the results of your spell may be much subtler than you ever could have imagined. Perhaps the change will be entirely internal, and you will simply become someone worthy of promotion. Maybe you will be granted reprieve from a particular expense, allowing you to save more in the long run. While winning the lottery is not impossible, do not expect that your spell will always work in this manner. Imagine how badly the pot would be split if everyone was granted this wish whenever they asked for it!

So long as you are not casting this spell solely out of avarice, you should yield results in one way or another. Identifying these gains when they come to you might be even trickier than casting your spell in the first place. Either way, make sure you know the difference between need and greed.

A person in need of money is not necessarily flat broke; sometimes a person just needs a little boost to overcome a financial hurdle.

The point is, do not expect to become extraordinarily wealthy with the wave of a hand and a few incantations. If you do not need vast wealth, or are not deserving of it, then you cannot expect this level of gain.

Money Talismans

Talismans are items which you have enchanted and can keep on your person to keep the magick flowing your way. Any number of various objects might suffice as your talisman, so long as you can keep the item on you at all times.

A talisman can be enchanted with just about any type of magick, though you may want to consider the correspondences of your chosen item to the purpose of your spell. This will increase the chances of drawing in success no matter where you are.

The following spells will help you to enchant items to use as money talismans. These charms will draw in positive attraction energies at all times, increasing your chances of success.

The Money Jar

While a number of items are needed for this spell, the procedure itself is simple and can be practiced repeatedly as a sort of daily mantra.

Necessities include:

• A relatively small, lidded container (a mason jar would work perfectly)

• 5 types of coin, differing in denomination or nationality

• 5 small lengths of cinnamon

• 5 dry corn kernels

• 5 sesame seeds

• 5 allspice seeds

• 5 dried cloves

• 5 peanuts

Note: The peanuts should not be salted and should not have shells. For the purpose of putting as much personal care as possible into this spell, you may wish to buy natural peanuts and de-shell them yourself.

Also, be careful regarding the size of the container. It should fit all of the necessities without too much surplus room. Remember that these items represent your incoming prosperity, so you don't want to fill the jar or bottle with nothing but air!

Fill your container with the other ingredients and close the lid. Shake it firmly as you repeat the following incantation:

"With spices and seeds
And coins for clarity,
I hastily seek
Increased prosperity."

You may desire to repeat this three times, or as many as it takes to feel as if the spell has taken hold.

Once you are done, you may keep the container near your workspace if you wish to continue putting your energy into its contents.

You may also try the following alternate incantation if you wish, especially if you are performing the spell out of need:

"With harvest provisions
And symbols of wealth,
I strengthen my vision
Of financial health."

High John's Bag of Luck

For this spell, you are going to want to seek out a New Age supplier or occult shop for the lucky hand root.

In most spells, ingredient substitutions can be used so long as the symbolism is there, but here the ingredients are precisely what give the talisman its power.

Supplies include:

- Small green bag (a folded bit of cloth will also do)

- lucky hand root piece

- High John root piece

- basil leaves (dried or fresh)

- 3 coins - silver

- String

Note: Make sure that you have solid pieces of each root. It is not a good idea either symbolically or magickally to use money-drawing roots which have been broken into little pieces.

Making this talisman is as simple as putting all of your ingredients into your bag (or into the centre of your bit of cloth) and tying the end closed with a string.

You will want to carry this on your person whenever possible, as you never know when an opportunity is lurking around the corner in which you just might benefit from an extra bit of luck.

Also pray on your charm bag nightly, keeping it constantly imbued with the power of your attraction energies.

Easy Tonka Bean Talisman

For this talisman, you only need a single ingredient:

- One whole Tonka bean

No joke. That is ALL you need. It might take a bit of footwork to find one, but consulting any local herbalists or occultists should greatly narrow the search.

The beauty of this talisman is that your only ingredient is one which is primarily used for money-drawing.

This fact should help boost your confidence as you charge your token with full knowledge that nature has begun the work for you.

All you have to do now is hold the bean in your hand while speaking the following incantation:

"When these words are spoken
With ardor and clarity,
This Tonka bean token
Will bring me prosperity."

Remember, do not stop repeating this enchantment until you are sure you BELIEVE it!

You might want to follow some advice from the last spell, keeping the token on you always and charging it before you retire at night.

Also keep in mind that these talismans are stronger when kept near your purse, wallet or money clip. To ensure you don't lose it or that nothing chips away at its surface, you might consider acquiring a small green bag to keep your token in while you carry it.

Money Magnet

This talisman does precisely what the name implies. You are going to charge a stone and carry it with you as you would with any other talisman. You will need:

- A few pieces of cinnamon stick

- 1 good piece of malachite

- A silver bowl

- Patchouli

- Pine oil

- Dill

Taking into account the correspondences we learned about earlier, you may want to make your talisman on a Thursday.

Begin by mixing your herbs in the silver bowl and mix in just a few drops of pine oil.

The amounts you use are not as important as the ingredients themselves, but you might want to go light on the pine oil and patchouli as both are quite strong in terms of smell.

When you are done mixing, place the stone in the centre of the bowl with the herbs all around it. Cover the bowl and let it charge on its own for seven days. On the following Thursday, take it out.

Keep the malachite in your pocket, but do not dispose of the herb mixture. Keep it somewhere safe, like your altar if you have one, until you start to reap the benefits of your new talisman.

Once you have started earning money, you may dispose of the herbs (preferably outside as opposed to the waste bin).

Magick by Moonlight

You'll need to perform this on the night of a full moon, and it should be fairly so the moonlight actually floods in through the window. Hopefully, you won't find that too inconvenient.

All you then need is:

• Water from a natural source (such as rain or spring water)

• 7 fresh leaves of basil

• Small cauldron

• 1 silver coin

Note: Even for those who frequent occult shops and New Age supply stores, a cauldron may not be the most common of household items.

If this is the case, a ceramic bowl may suffice. The coin must actually contain silver, so possibly look for an older sixpence or U.S. dime.

Start by placing the coin inside of the bowl or cauldron, as centered as you can get it. Pour natural water over the coin until the cauldron is half full (or more, if you so desire).

Place the bowl or cauldron on a table or windowsill where it will be exposed to moonlight.

Drop the basil leaves into the water individual (not all at once) as you say the following:

"Water and moonlight,
Silver and leaf,
Please grant me blessings,
Wealth and relief."

Let the cauldron remain where it is overnight, then pour the ingredients outside the following morning. Keep the coin to carry around in your pocket.

When One Door Closes...

Another presents itself. But why close any doors at all? Here's what you will need to start leaving them all open:

• A banknote (try to use a $20/£20 note, or possibly even something bigger)

• 5 twigs of pine, around the same length for each

•Green and silver ribbon (or yarn)

•Patchouli oil

Note: The twigs should be on the smaller side, but should not be pine needles.

Place the banknote on your altar/table first, then lay the twigs on top of it. The reason it might be preferable to use an altar space of this spell is that you will be letting the money and pine twigs sit there for a full week before continuing the spell.

Once a week has passed, rub each twig with a small amount of patchouli oil.

For each twig, repeat the following:

"Each of these twigs
I, with oil, caress
And open the doorway
To wealth and success."

Use your ribbon or yarn to bundle the twigs together into a small charm. You will want to leave some extra length of ribbon on the end to make a loop so that you can hang the charm from your front door.

You might hang it from the knob, though you might prefer a nail over the doorway. It does not technically matter if your charm hangs on the inside or the outside.

Let it hang there for a while, until the doors of success begin to open for you. Once this happens, you can take it down. You may wish to wait a week and then make another charm to keep doorways opening continuously.

Finance by Five

This spell uses a correspondence which is often ignored: that of numbers. The number associated with prosperity and abundance of wealth is the number "5."

You will not need much for this, only the following:

• Green, non-permanent marker (silver will also do if necessary)

• Silver coin

Go ahead and do this on Thursday, which is the fifth day of the week starting from Sunday.

Use the marker to draw a little number "1" on your index finger and count up across the rest of them so that "4" is on the pinkie. The "5" will be on your thumb.

Concentrate strongly on your motivations behind doing this spell, transferring that energy into the coin.

Once you are satisfied, place the coin on your table or altar but do not let go of your concentration.

This spell is largely need-based, so try to focus on the reasons you must use magick rather than "normal" means of gain.

Touch the coin with your fingers in numbered order, as you recite the following verse:

"On touch of one, the spell has begun.
On touch of two, the spell becomes true.
On touch of three, good tidings shall be.
On touch of four, I'm granted more.
On touch of five, my magick's alive."

Once you have finished, open your hand and place the whole of your palm over the silver coin. Once again, repeat these lines (without the finger touches).

Carry this talisman on you at all times, but not immediately after finishing the spell; for maximum effect, you will want to let the coin stay where it is for five days and start carrying it once this time has passed.

Welcoming New Wealth

This is different from the previous talismans, as you will not be keeping it on your person. It is more of a charm for the household itself.

This spell is for your doormat. Your magickally enhanced welcome mat will require some extra supplies, including:

- A welcome mat (new or old, though you might prefer a new one)

- Patchouli (in herb form, not the oil)

- Chips of sandalwood

- Dry basil leaves

- A silver coin

Make sure your welcome mat is placed where you would like it to remain once your spell is done.

Lift it up and sprinkle your three herbs on the ground beneath it. Put your silver coin in the centre of the mixture and put the welcome mat back where it was.

Stand on top of it while facing north and repeat the following at least three times:

"Good tidings are welcome, there's no need to knock.
Success and good wealth, keep this house in good stock.
This mat is the herald of fortune's advance.
Let it take the front door, and please make a loud entrance."

Let the mat (and coin) remain. Fortune will come to you, so long as you continue putting out the proper energies.

Candle Magick

for Wealth & Success

When many people think of magick, they will conjure up images of candles, an alter and robes. While not necessities, candles can help your magick tremendously.

They focus and train your energy into a single and powerful thought.

These prosperity spells will help you attract some extra money, just don't use them just for your own greed.

They probably won't work very well if you decide to do that. Earth is the association of all prosperity spells involving money.

Pay Your Bills

Many spells have various uses, but this one is very particular. If you're a debtor, or behind on your bills, this spell should work for you.

If you're simply trying to get rich, look elsewhere. Here is what you'll need to make this work:

- Green candle and a candleholder (silver, if possible)

- Cinnamon oil or patchouli oil

- Incense of same aroma as oil

- Piece of paper

- Pen or pencil

With your paper and writing utensil, draw or write something that represents the bill. You might draw something that stands for the utility you're paying off whatever it was that got you into debt (such as a horse or a card suit if you're a gambler).

Conversely, you might just write out what it is.

Drawing is recommended, as the creative energy it takes will put that much more attraction energy into the spell.

You can also make a copy of the bill, but this will put the least amount of energy into your spell.

Whatever you do, DO NOT USE THE ACTUAL BILL. Not unless you can pay it online, anyway, since you're going to be burning your paper.

Use the oils to anoint your candle. Fold the paper and then put it in the base of the candleholder with the candle on top of it (make sure the candle is secure over the paper and will not fall out).

Light the incense, followed by the candle. Keep your focus on the centre of the flames as best you can as you recite the following:

"Candle burning
Oh so bright,
Clear my debts,
Set all wrongs right."

As you recite this, make sure your focus stays on the nature of your bill or debt.

Spend about fifteen minutes meditating on how you fell behind on this payment and why you need to rectify the situation.

After these fifteen minutes, put out the flame.

You are going to want to use a candle large enough to burn for about an hour and forty-five minutes, as you will be repeating this fifteen-minute process of meditation for another six days (so a week in total).

On the seventh day, take the paper out from under the candle and hold it over the flame so that it burns. Then let the candle burn to completion.

Don't forget that you have performed this spell. If any sudden income should come your way, put it toward the bill instead of to personal use. Otherwise, the magick will be wasted and your karma might suffer for it.

Elemental Earnings

This spell is not too complicated, yet holds the benefit of including all four major elements in its casting. Gather the following before you begin:

- Green candle

- Sage incense

- Water

- Salt

You may want to use the corresponding directions as you put each element to work. You will want to go clockwise (deasil), as counter-clockwise (widdershins) is commonly considered to undo magick.

As you light the incense, face the East:

"Guardians of air, watchtowers of the East, bring me the wisdom to spend my money wisely."

As you light the candle, face the South:

"Guardians of fire, watchtowers of the South, grant me the strength to reach success."

While drinking a small bit of water, face the West. Then say:

"Guardians of water, watchtowers of the West, cleanse all negativity to bring in good fortune."

While putting a small bit of salt on your tongue, face the North. Then say:

"Guardians of earth, watchtowers of the North, steel my resolve to find new wealth."

It is not required, but you may wish to once again perform the circle, this time without words.

When you are done, stomp the ground with your right foot and firmly speak these words:

"This rite is ended, but the circle is unbroken. So mote it be."

Allow the candle and the incense to continue burning until finished. Do not remove the elemental items from your altar until the magick has begun to bring new tidings your way.

This means leave out the ash from the incense, the stub and melted wax from the candle, and small bowls or containers for the water and salt.

Since magick takes time and water evaporates, these items may need some maintenance until the spell has taken hold.

Wax-Covered Token of Wealth

With most candle magick, you want to put a decent amount of visual concentration on the flame.

In this case, visualize yourself drawing in money and emanating success the same way the flame emanates light and heat. You will need:

• Green candle and candleholder (wide enough to fit a coin in the bottom)

• A key or other sharp/edged object to carve into the candle

• A coin of large denomination

• Vanilla extract or oil

• Cinnamon oil

Take your key or other edged object and carve into the side of the candle.

You will want to spell the word "wealth" or "success," or you can even do both if the candle is wide enough to write on both sides. Once this is done, use the vanilla and cinnamon oils to anoint your candle on all sides.

In the bottom of the candleholder, place the coin with the candle on top of it. Light the candle and set it somewhere it will not blow out. You want it to finish burning in one go if possible.

Your coin will then be covered in the wax of your anointed candle, and will become a talisman of sorts.

Keep it somewhere safe, maybe somewhere you will notice it so that you can meditate on it daily until the spell has begun to work.

Ringing in New Tidings

Silver bells are more than just a symbol of Christmastime in the city. With this spell, you'll be sounding good cheer as you rake in the abundant fruits of your magick.

First gather the following:

- Silver or white candle

- 3 green candles

- 4 candleholders

- Silver bell

- Pine oil

Use the pine oil to anoint all of the candles, as well as your hands. Set each one in a candleholder (as always, silver if possible) and then arrange these on your table or altar.

You will want the silver or white candle in the centre of the arrangement with the green ones forming a triangle around it.

Light the three green candles and then ring the silver bell three times as you recite:

"Ring three times,
Ye bells that shine.
Sing three times
Of wealth now mine."

Now it is time to light the silver/white candle before ringing the bell three more times and speaking these words:

"Ring three times,
Attract success.
Sing three times
Of life now blessed."

Do not snuff out the candles, but allow them to burn through.

As with most other spells, it is advisable to leave these items on your altar until you have begun to see new wealth and success enter into your life.

Sweet Dreams of Success

You may wonder if there's a way to make the lessons you've learned about visualization in this book continue to work for you in your sleep.

It can absolutely be done, and this spell will help. It will also potentially help you to have dreams that will influence your decision-making in a way that leads you to new success.

Your ingredients this time include:

• A small green bag or cloth that can be made into a bag

• A pillow you can sleep on every night

• A few drops of pine oil

• Green candle

• Patchouli

•Mugwort

• Lavender

- Cedar

- Mint

- Dill

First, put all of the herbs into your small green bag or cloth sachet. The amount of each herb does not matter, but try to keep them somewhat equal.

Above all, make sure you do not leave anything out.

Next, anoint your pillow with the pine oil. Light the green candle, possibly somewhere in your bedroom where you can focus on the flame as you fall asleep, but definitely somewhere it will be safe to burn out overnight.

Finally, simply put your herb bag underneath your anointed pillow and try to do some visualization exercises as you fall into slumber.

You should find yourself having dreams

which will inspire you to make better decisions, or at the very least will strengthen your resolve in becoming a more successful person.

Money from the Darkness

You might be familiar with the concept that you shouldn't wear black in hot weather because it attracts the heat energy of the sun.

Well, you can use that attraction to draw in other forms of energy as well, including the attraction energies needed to build wealth and success.

Do this spell on a day which corresponds to a celestial body that may aid your magick. The best days are Sunday (the sun), Thursday (Jupiter), or Friday (Venus).

Here is what you'll need:

• Sharp or edged object for carving into wax

•2 black candles

Begin by carving words into your candles that you associate with wealth or success. You may also use monetary symbols.

Also, include your name on one side of each candle.

Light each candle and grip them both tightly. Your grip should be tight enough that you can feel the energy of your heart pulsing through your fingertips.

Concentrate on your aura and try to connect with the energy of the candles' flames. Let your power flow through the flames, using the candles as your transistors.

Use the visualization techniques you have learned from this book to concentrate on what you are trying to achieve, and recite the following words:

"Oh power divine,
Let new wealth be mine
Let my success and my influence grow strong.
I ask of these flames
Earnings under my name
While doing no karmic wrong."

Snuff out the flame. Do not blow it out, for you do not want to introduce a new element to this spell.

Perform this ritual nightly until the candles are completely burned through.

This will not only increase the benefits of the magick, but also your abilities of concentration and visualization.

Simple Money Magick

None of the above spells have been "hard," per se. Still, you may wish for a spell which requires a little less concentration or time. If you are in a bind or trying to make money fast, this is fairly understandable.

It's always best when you can put more work in, but some people simply don't have the time or energy. Others simply lack to experience to focus properly.

For those people, the following spells will prove useful. Simply because more time and energy will benefit a spell does not mean that simple magick won't work at all.

Simple magick is sometimes desirable for a quick-but-effective ritual.

Do not think of "simple" as meaning "uneducated" or "dumb." This spells may lack complexity, but brevity is sometimes more important than an elaborate rite.

This especially applies to a beginner who is overworked at the office and doesn't have much time to spare on magick rituals.

They can also help those who do not have time to work with corresponding moon phases or days of the week.

If the above paragraphs describe you, try using any one of these spells for a quick boost of income or success.

Visualization Bath

This is a great spell to use right before a networking event, or maybe the morning or night before you're being considered for a promotion.

It can also be great when interviewing for a job or taking out a loan.

Simply decide the best time to perform this spell and gather the following items:

- Small bottle or other lidded container

- A small dash of patchouli (herb form)

- A decent handful of sea salt

- 3 drops of cinnamon oil

- 3 drops of basil oil

- 3 drops of pine oil

Fill your bathtub with warm water. Mix in all ingredients and try to stir the water a bit with your hand. Bathe in the mixture for about a quarter of an hour while visualizing the event for which you are preparing. Use the techniques in previous chapters to achieve optimal visualization of gains to come.

Picture yourself getting ready for the event, and follow through to the outcome you want to see realized.

Once you have completed your visualization and the requisite amount of time has passed, you can drain the tub. Do not do so, however, without first filling your container with the water.

This water contains not only the herbal concoction you have mixed into it, but also the energy you have put out during your meditation.

You can now carry the bottle or vial with you as a talisman to aid your chances of achieving your visualized outcome.

Harvest Husk Wealth Spell

As with the other simple magick spells in this book, you can cast this spell at any time. If you are able, however, you may wish to wait until the harvest season.

Here is what you will need:

- Dried leaf of corn husk (flattened to the best of your ability)

- A small banknote ($1/£5)

- Green yarn or ribbon

- Patchouli oil

Anoint the inside of the corn leaf with oil as you recite this incantation:

"I now commence this harvest spell
To cultivate success and wealth.
Bring gains to me,
So mote it be.
With this rite, all be well."

As you speak these words, focus on a life of wealth and success as well as good health and happiness. This is a harvest spell, so the energy you put out is the energy you will cultivate later.

When you are done with the recitation, roll the banknote into the husk leaf. Use your yarn or ribbon to tie the two into a cylindrical bundle, leaving a loop at the end so you can hang your new charm above the front door or on the doorknob.

Then sit back and wait for new gains to spring forth.

Powerfully Potent Potpourri

Not only does this spell not take much time, but you will be forming a mixture which can be spread throughout the household in bowls and other containers.

You can even increase the amounts in the ingredients list to make a nice gift for friends on whom you wish good tidings!

It will double not only as a gift of magick but also a very nice fragrance for any room.

If you want to increase the power of this mixture, try putting it into bowls using colors such as green, silver or gold.

Either way, you will need the following:

• A few handfuls of dried flowers or flower petals (Echinacea, hibiscus, lily, tulip, hyacinth, violet, and narcissus all work well)

• 1 tsp of ground cinnamon (or some equal lengths of cinnamon stick, if desired)

• Patchouli oil or vetiver oil (or both, if possible)

- 1 handful of cedar shavings

- 1 tsp ground nutmeg

Note: While the flowers listed above are preferred, it is really up to your personal preference. Your positive energy is much more important than your ingredients, though you should still try to include at least one or two of these flowers if you can.

Lily and tulip will likely be the easiest to acquire.

Combine all ingredients into a bowl, multiplying the amounts depending on how much potpourri you plan to make.

Do not add the oil until you are satisfied with the mixture.

You may need to do this once a month to keep your concoction fresh. Until then, keep some spare oil on hand to add to the bowl(s) whenever you sense the aroma beginning to fade.

This can be done any time of year, but spring is the best season as it will signal new growth.

Planting the Seeds of Success

The plant you use for this spell does not matter, though it never hurts to find one which corresponds magickally with your desired goals.

You will not need much for this. All you need is:

• A living plant (preferably a jade plant, basil plant, lily or tulip)

• A small dash of patchouli (herb, not oil)

• 1 coin of any denomination

Like the spell above, this is a great spell to do in the spring. Make sure to pick a healthy plant, either one that is still growing or one that has thrived to full health.

If you are not pressed for time, you might even wish to grow a new seed.

Whether your plant is potted or in a garden (you may prefer it to be potted so as to keep it safe from the weather), you will want to sprinkle some of your patchouli around it. Then place your coin into the soil near the base of the plant and press it down.

You want a little bit of the coin to stick out, but you might still consider sprinkling some more patchouli on top.

If you want to use a coin of a larger denomination, you absolutely can.

The reason you want it sticking out of the dirt is that you will be taking the coin out and spending it whenever the spell has brought some extra wealth or success your way.

You will then repeat the ritual, putting another coin in the soil (along with another plant, if the first has started to wither) and maybe even sprinkling on some more patchouli.

In between repetitions of this ritual process, tend to your plant as best you can.

Never forget that in doing so, you are also tending to the power of the magickal energy with which you have imbued its growth.

The Five-Knotted Banknote

This is one of the simplest spells in this book. You will only need the following to make this work:

- A banknote of any denomination

- Green ribbon or yarn

- Pine oil

Coat the yarn or ribbon with oil, then tie five knots (as evenly spaced as possible) down the length of it. With each knot, you will say one line of the following:

"By knot of one, this rite hath begun.
By knot of two, my words cometh true.
By knot of three, so mote it be.
By knot of four, success is in store.
By knot of five, my wealth shall thrive."

Note: If you are somewhat experienced and have worked with cord magick in the past, you will recognize this as a money-based variation on the "Spell of Nine Knots," which is common amongst those who are initiated into the craft. That does not mean you have to be initiated to perform this particular spell, as it has been altered for your benefit.

When you are done speaking the incantation, wrap the knotted length of yarn or ribbon around the banknote so that they form what looks like a little scroll.

This will take a little bit of finesse, as you do not want the banknote to become unrolled, but you also do not want to add another knot to the length of yarn or ribbon.

Since you will not be tying another knot, you will not be hanging this above the door. Instead, put it somewhere it will not be disturbed. If you have one, your altar will be the best bet.

Otherwise, you might consider putting it somewhere it will be exposed to your positive attraction energies, such as a safe spot around your workspace.

No-Fail Money Spells

There has been a lot of talk in this book about the most effective way to cast your magick, and what will or will not make a spell work best.

You can't form expectations that you will turn into Donald Trump or J.K. Rowling overnight, but you should not consider these things outside the realm of possibility, either. This balance of your expectations can be difficult to maintain.

These spells may not promise you millions of dollars overnight, but like all money magick this can still be a possibility if you are deserving of it.

Either way, these spells will yield some results, whether it is a small bonus on your pay-check or even a simple gift card from a relative that got lost in the mail. Without fail, you will see results either big or small.

Apple and Athame

An athame is a ritual dagger that practicing magicians may work with quite often; others, however, may be completely unfamiliar with them.

Don't fret if you are part of the latter group, as you can use a simple knife for this spell.

Even those who own a wide array of ritual tools may wish to opt for this, as many prefer not to use their athame for cutting under any circumstances.

The choice is yours. In any case, you will need:

- An athame or sharp knife

- 1 green apple (uncut)

- 5 whole cloves

Take your blade and lightly carve a pentacle (a pentagram with a circle around it) into the surface. Be as gentle as possible, trying to break the skin without actually cutting the fruit. You might want to cut a little deeper near the points of the star, trying to bore little holes into them.

Place each clove in one of these holes. Try to press it as deep as you can so that it is visible but not sticking out (you want it to stay in).

Take your newly decorated apple in your right hand and face north as you recite these words:

"I ask the earth to grant this fruit
The power of success, and wealth to boot.
I place my energy into each clove,
And pray that prosperity finds my home."

Note: You might consider drawing a pentagram in the air with your blade as your recite these words. Start at the top point, moving the blade down to your right.

You will end with an upward motion back to the top, at which point you can draw a circle with a clockwise motion to complete the invisible seal.

Set the apple down on your altar. Repeat the incantation, drawing another seal in the air if you wish.

This time, upon completion, you will want to drive your blade into the top of the apple. Hit as close to dead centre as you can.

Leave your apple and athame/knife on the altar as they are for about twenty-four hours.

If you are doing this spell in the morning, you may simply leave them until that evening before removing the blade (dusk is a good time to complete the spell, as it is a time of transition).

Remove the cloves if you wish and eat the apple while visualizing increased wealth and success.

Attraction Energy Tea

This spell has the benefit of being easy to repeat as often as you wish.

It can be a daily ritual, a one-time affair, or something that you do on days which are particularly powerful for success and money magick (Friday, Sunday, and especially Thursday).

Any evening on which you prefer to work your magick, gather the following ingredients:

- Small dash of dried dill weed

- ½ tbsp. of dried basil

- Ground cinnamon

- Honey

Note: There are really no precise amounts, even with the basil. You can experiment with this recipe until you have found a mixture to suit your tastes.

Boil some water and pour it into a teacup, steeping the dill weed and basil for approximately ten minutes.

Given the texture of the ingredients, you are definitely going to want to use a tea strainer if you have one.

You will wind up with a rather bitter liquid, so add as much honey and cinnamon as you desire.

Try to lean toward more cinnamon, as it is an ingredient used in other money spells as well.

If you can, take some time out of your day to meditate while you drink this tea. You will find yourself overflowing with attraction energy as you repeat this ritual more and more.

It's as simple as it is effective, so there's no harm in doing this every day if you have the time and ingredients.

The Jar of Hope

This is a preferred spell for those seeking magick which is both powerfully effective as well as easy to perform. All you will need for this is:

- A quart-sized bottle or jar with a lid that screws on

- 7 silver coins

- 1 bay leaf

- A bit of paper

- Pen or pencil

Think over what precisely you hope to gain from this spell and then write it on your piece of paper before placing it in the jar or bottle.

Then, using your right hand (or left hand, if that is your dominant one), drop each coin individual coin into the container.

Practice your visualization techniques while dropping each coin. You want to imagine each coin multiplying into larger and larger amounts, so it doesn't hurt to use coins of a large denomination.

As you drop each coin, speak these words:

"These tokens, they do symbolize
Gains to appear before my eyes.
These tokens they will grow to be
The tools of my prosperity."

Now, on the back of the bay leaf, inscribe your name and let it fall on top of the coins. Affix the lid to the top of the jar or bottle and you are done!

That said, you do not have to stop there if you do not wish to do so.

You want to keep the jar in a safe place, but somewhere you will see it frequently so that it will become a focal point during your daily meditations/visualizations.

Since you want it to be full of your own energy, consider making this a spot in your bedroom or somewhere else that not every visitor to your abode will be able to see it.

You can add one or two coins on a daily basis, repeating the incantation if you wish.

Once you have started to attain money, success, or whatever else you have wished for on your sheet of paper, you can remove the wish paper and bury it in your garden or some other safe spot (such as a potted plant, possibly one relating to money magick like a basil or jade plant).

After the wish has been removed, you can remove the other items as well. You might bury the leaf with the paper, and you might spend the coins so that your energy continues to flow throughout the world.

Keep the jar, for it might make a great vessel if you wish to repeat this spell to fulfill another wish.

Conclusion

Continuing Your Magickal Journey

You have now learned a great deal about money magick, visualizing success, some various types of spells and many spells of each type.

This, however, is only the beginning of your education in the world of money magick.

Hopefully the spells you have learned here,

in conjunction with the chapter on how to customize your own magick, will help you to grow stronger in the ways of the universe and learn how to perform rituals of your own creation.

This will come in time, with much effort. For some it will take much longer than others.

Do not get discouraged. If magick were easy, everyone would do it. That said, since you are depending on your own energies, it will ultimately be up to you whether or not this journey is a difficult one. It may take many readings of this book to fully soak in its teachings.

You may wish to combine these teachings with other research to expand your knowledge.

In this research, try to concentrate on ingredients and correspondences more than anything.

You may find that some will suit your needs better than others. If you are interested in evoking the gods in your workings, you will find no shortage of deities for each purpose.

This does not just apply to Wiccans, either. The Bible and other monotheistic literature is rife with angels, saints, and other such powerful individuals with the ability to help you in your journey.

This may influence how you perform your meditations or visualizations. Some may not be religious at all, and simply wish to harness the energy all around them.

Whoever you are, always do some daily inventory to make sure your moral intentions have not been overwhelmed with avaricious desire. If you are meek, you shall inherit.

If you are greedy and malicious, then you will suffer the consequences of errant magick.

Above all else, attempt to enjoy every step of the way. At times, your circumstances may be trying. That does not mean you cannot benefit from the life lessons which are present all around you.

If you tap into the energies which linger in the air about you, there is virtually no end to the level of wisdom and abundance which you can achieve.

May your life be enriched with good tidings of your own making. Blessed be!

GABRIEL ARCHER

ABOUT THE AUTHOR

Gabriel Archer, a practicing occultist, has been a teacher of magick for 15 years.

He has published several books on the subject, including subjects such as love magick, health spells and prosperity books.

He lives in Rumford, Maine, with wife Julia, three kids and two dogs.

CPSIA information can be obtained at www.ICGtesting.com
Printed in the USA
LVOW08s1435280616

494433LV00001B/31/P